MAD
BAD
Dangerously
HADDOCK

Andrew Fusek Peters has written and edited over 45 books for children, many with his wife Polly Peters. Two of their verse collections were nominated for the Carnegie Medal and another anthology is now part of the National Curriculum. Many of the poems in *Mad, Bad and Dangerously Haddock* feature on Andrew's CD for the Poetry Archive (www.poetryarchive.org), set up by the Poet Laureate to record the best poems for children and adults.

Andrew has performed and led workshops in schools and at festivals for over 20 years, entertaining audiences with his didgeridoo, juggling and mad poems. He has also performed and written for TV, including BBC's *Wham Bam Strawberry Jam* and *Blue Peter*, and his radio work includes Radio 4's *Talking Poetry* and poems on *Poetry Please*.

Mad, Bad and Dangerously Haddock draws on the best of Andrew's previous four collections for younger readers, work that has appeared in anthologies and a whole new set of material. More information about his boo'

In memory of my brother Mark Edward Peters,
a fine poet, and to Dorothy McNeill at Sherbourne
who first published my poems all those years ago.

MAD, Bad' and Dangerously HADDOCK...

ANDREW FUSEK PETERS

Illustrated by

Alastair Stevens

LION
CHILDREN'S

Text copyright © 2006 Andrew Fusek Peters
Illustrations copyright © 2006 Alastair Stevens
This edition copyright © 2006 Lion Hudson

The moral rights of the author and illustrator
have been asserted

A Lion Children's Book
an imprint of
Lion Hudson plc
Mayfield House, 256 Banbury Road,
Oxford OX2 7DH, England
www.lionhudson.com
ISBN-13: 978-0-7459-6021-0
ISBN-10: 0-7459-6021-9

First edition 2006
10 9 8 7 6 5 4 3 2 1 0

A catalogue record for this book is available
from the British Library

Typeset in 11.5/14 Zapf Humanist BT
Printed and bound in Great Britain
by Cox and Wyman Ltd, Reading

Contents

Poem for the Verbally Confused

Got up, Boiled the bed,
Took a train downstairs,
Feeling live-tired and with such a baking head.

Drank not one shredded wheat but three,
Then I Grew myself a nice cup of tea,
Planted some toast, Watered the eggs,
Sat down in a chair and Ate my legs.

Crushed my teeth, Smashed my face,
Poached my hair 'til I Looked dead ace!
Dug my way to school,
And after Went for a Snog in the local Snogging Pool!

Caught the bus, Put it in my pocket,
My mum Made a fuss and Told me to Return it.
Killed my homework, which Was very Satisfying,
Especially when all the answers Were Writhing around
   and Dying!

In the end, I Pounded into bed,
Cut off my tired and weary head
And Swam down deep into soft and silent sleep...

Late for a Date

Toasty dreams have crumbled away,
To the cornflake dawn of day,
Birds sing loud as a kettle on the boil,
I wriggle from bed like a worm out of soil.
As sunlight pours a cup of tea
The mist is rising, just like me,
Shiver like a fridge, wait in the queue,
Traffic jam outside the loo.
Clothes laid out like butter on bread,
Squeeze them on like sandwich spread!
Hungry as a horse, maybe too late
Gallop downstairs, await my fate.
Mum looks sour, but Dad's so sweet,
He saved my bacon! Time to eat!

The Melodramatic Kid

My sulks are known of far and wide
And stars are jealous of the way I sigh.
If they say it's just a little scratch
I know that I'm going to die.

I have a PhD in pouting,
I'm an expert in stomping up stairs,
And Wow! The way that I slam that door
Because nobody ever cares!

Thank you, no really, you're too kind,
I must ask you to stop the applause,
For driving my parents up the wall
Is a most deserving cause.

I am able to run my tears like a tap,
Please admire my sorrowful face.
If there was a prize for tantrums,
Yours truly would take first place!

Mum

She's a:

Sadness stealer
Cut knee healer
Hug-me-tighter
Wrongness righter
Gold star carer
Chocolate sharer
(well, sometimes!)

Hamster feeder
Bedtime reader
Great game player
Night fear slayer
Treat dispenser
Naughtiness sensor
(how come she always knows?)

She's my
Never glum
Constant chum
Second to none
We're under her thumb!
Mum!

Dad

He's a:

Tall story weaver
Full of fib fever
Bad joke teller
Ten-decibel yeller
Baggy clothes wearer
Pocket money bearer
Nightmare banisher
Hurt heart vanisher

Bear hugger
Biscuit mugger
Worry squasher
Noisy nosher
Lawn mower
Smile sower

He's my
Football mad
Fashion sad
Not half bad
So glad I had my
Dad!

Hey Diddle Diddle

'Wash your ears!' Mum said.
So I took them off,
And stuck them in the washing machine.

'Clean your room!' Dad said.
So I rolled it up,
And shook it out of the window.

'Make the breakfast!' my brother said.
So I did –
With bits of balsa wood and modelling glue.

'Feed the cat!' my auntie said.
So I fed him...
To the dog!

'Take your time!' Dad said.
So I packed up the clocks
And flew off to Mars
Where the days fly by,
Wearing nothing but stars!

In Training

The train is at Born-Ville station.
The whistle wails and we're off to
    Nappily-Ever-After Land.
It's a Poo-Poo train, making its way to Crawley.
All change for Childhood-On-The-Daughter.
Now we are nearly at Little Tantrum.
But things are not going our way.
The train speeds on to Big Tantrum.
The brakes screech and scream to an unscheduled stop.
There is an argument on the line,
And we are so close to the town of Kiss-And-Make-Up,
Suddenly diverted to Sulkington-On-See-Me-Later.
We might have to bypass Middle Pudding and
Head straight to Bed-Stone.
At last we have arrived at TV station.
Passengers are advised to watch out for rubbish.
Thank you for travelling on our one-to-five express!

Fairynuff?

We walk to the edge of the stream,
And Dad lifts me high
And plops me on the other side
Where the old oak stands on tiptoe,
Trying to reach the sky,
Dressed in a bark-jigsaw.
'Look, a fairy-hole!' says Dad.
I push my stick in and jig it about.
'You don't want to do that,
The fairies might be having a snooze!'
So I take my stick out and peer right in –
It's dark and smells a bit musty, like Grandad.
'I can't see anything!' I say.
'They are masters of disguise!' he replies.
'Hmmm!' I say, 'Well, they're no fun then.'

We leave the fairies to have a lie-in
And get to work on the stream,
Lifting stones, plugging the gaps with moss
And watching the water rise to make a pool.
'Fancy a swim?' says Dad.
'Daaad!' I say, stretching his name out for miles,
  'It's cold!'
And it is, as the water pours over the top of my wellies
And I'm stuck like a statue.
The mud slurps and gloops as Dad's huge hands pull
  me out.
We say goodbye to the water,
Wave to the sleeping fairies
And Dad lifts me high in my wet socks
Onto his sky-scraping shoulders.
Our breaths turn into clouds
As we sway our way home
To the fire, and jam on crumpets with tea.

Thank You (it's what I've always wanted)

Dear Auntie,
Thanks for the hand-knitted cloud.
It will come in useful on sunny days,
Though the grey colour has left me feeling
A bit under the weather.

Dear Uncle,
I'm not too sure how to feed a star?
And it was difficult to sleep last night
(On account of the star being so bright).

Dear Grandma,
Wow! My very own river! What can I say?
I did try to fold it up in my cupboard, but it leaked
and Mum had to call a plumber.

Dear Cousin,
I am writing... to... thank... you... for...
the... mountain
(sorry, am... out of breath... climbing
over it... to get...
the pencil out of my... drawer).

Dear Grandad,
It was very thoughtful of you
to give me my own city.
It's what I've always wanted.
There is a slight problem though with
squeezing 11 million people
into my room (and I won't even
mention all the buildings!)
but nevertheless,
Thank you.

Morning

(in memory of Jana Fusek)

The whole house hums with sleep
As me and my brother tumble like leaves
Downstairs,
Scattering night.
In the living room,
Half-light creeps through blinds.
We fight to the death over Grandad's chair.
I win and recline most royally on this, his throne by day.
My brother wakes the sleeping box,
He waves the aerial like a sword
In the battle with fuzz...
Until, at last,
We can feast on the candy of cartoons.

Grandma Babi is suddenly there,
Stern and so small
You could fold her away in a drawer.
We practise our pleading,
For underneath her no-nonsense frown
There lurks a smile and we know it.
Soon, a smell tiptoes in from the kitchen,
Taunting noses and teasing empty stomachs.
Grandma Babi is magic,
The conjurer of crispy bacon!
She kisses us each on the forehead,
And this blessing makes her wrinkles vanish,
Fills her face with a land she left long ago.

I am six and my brother is ten.
This time will never come again.

Grandad

My grandad in his suit and tie
Looks smart as a button. And I

Lean over to kiss him. He was so old,
His face like a wrinkled leaf now cold.

Perhaps he has gone off to sleep,
Leaving Mum and me to weep.

His soul's a blackbird, watch it fly
Free from his grand old suit and tie.

At the Top of the Stairs

I live at the top of the stairs,
The safest place to be,
Especially when there's an argument
In my stormy family.

It starts off in the living room,
It isn't very polite,
Their whisper grows into thunder,
I'm glad I'm out of sight.

I hate it when they shout,
It fills me up with gloom,
I hope the hurricane stays below
As I run to the safe of my room.

I think that they forget about me,
And my space at the top of the stairs,
Oh when will the storm blow over?
I wonder if anyone cares?

Peace

Peace is when I'm up first thing. The house is all hushed.
The fridge hums and the birds go doolally outside.
That's peace.

Peace happens during silent reading after lunch,
when the whole class is lost in a maze of amazing words.
That's peace.

Peace is when I hold my little brother in the pool.
His legs whirl like windmills
and I can feel his heart going BADOM! BADOM! BADOM!
That's peace.

Peace comes after play in the park,
with my friends on the bench,
out of breath but full of beans.
We swap jokes and smiles wriggle around our lips.
That's peace.

Peace is when Mum and Dad stop being grouchy
and do that yucky kiss-and-make-up stuff.
Even the house sighs and settles down.
That's peace.

Peace lies in wait at the end of the day
when Dad's just read me the best book ever.
As his footsteps pad away,
I sink down and think big thoughts.
That's peace.

The Chip Shop Wrap

Starving! Beg my dad for dosh,
Skip out the door and dream of nosh.

Wind outside, sharp and nippy
Toasty-warm inside the chippy.

In the queue – *come on, please!*
Salt and vinegar, mushy peas

Wrapped in a wrapper, oh what a pain,
Fight my way through bullying rain.

Finally home, shivering cold,
But on the plate lies steaming gold.

Delicious, just can't get enough
Of this crunchy, munchy stuff.

Sticky fingers, greasy lips,
Give a hand to Fish and Chips!

Junk Uncle

Bless Uncle Bert, untidy twit
So fond of trash, he lived in it,
In love with litter, master of mess,
How did he end up? Have a guess!
Picked up by the rubbish man,
Chucked in the back of the refuse van,
Uncle Bert, to dirt attracted,
Ended his days somewhat compacted.

Wriggle Bottom

I'm a fidget, I admit
This poor old body can't stop it.
In class or even dinner time
It moves to the rhythm of an itchy rhyme.

Fingers playing with my hair,
Those feet, they shuffle everywhere;
My wriggly bum is gonna go far,
It slides around like a football star.

I'm twitchy, itchy, can't sit still,
Hate it when there's time to kill,
'Cos I'm a fidget, can't you see,
Full of beans, that's right, that's me!

My Cat

My cat is a curled-up comma,
Paused on the bed as she purrs.

When my cat yawns,
She stretches out in a long, thin sentence,
Looks at me dot dot dot

Then turns into a humming simile,
Rubs against my shoes like polish
Until I fill her bowl to a full stop.

Then my cat is a sudden – dash –
She leaps on a ball of string,
All verb and hidden clause
Until the air is a flurry of exclamation marks!!!

Yes, my cat's the best, she's all right by me.
Her name? Of course, Apostrophe.

E-pet-aph

Gerbil Gerry made a mess
When he got trapped in the trouser press.
It's sad to say, the truth is that
Both of us now feel quite flat.
Poor old pet with a permanent crease,
Gerry Gerbil, Pressed In Peace.

Snoring

My brother's snoring
Makes such a sound!
It shakes the bed
And shivers the ground
I never get any sleep,
Not even a peep
Because of that creep…

So I stick my two big toes
Right up his nose!
It's the best way to stop him, I've found!

The River of Tears

Why is there rain, and where does it come from, Mum?
And how come clouds live up in the sky?
And why did my brother get ill and die?

The rain is a river of tears, my dear,
For every cloud sees how sad we are here.
Yet I don't know why your brother should die.

Why are the leaves so bright and so green, Mum
And how do they learn to fall off and fly?
And why did my brother get ill and die?

Leaves are alive and filled with breath, my child.
At the end of the year, they have their death.
But I just don't know how my son could die.

And will he ever come back again, Mum?
And can't we find him if we really try?
And I'm so unhappy, Mum, why did he die?

He's taken a boat to the river of tears
And we shall not see him for so many years.
So hold my hand, little one, and wave him goodbye.
So hold my hand tight, little one, and wave him goodbye.

It's Treason!

I'm a secret agent;
At school there is a Me,
My mum would never recognize
This strange identity.

I'm helpful and good-natured,
Excessively polite.
Yes, in my teacher's eyes,
I'm a star that shines out bright.

But when the learning's over,
And after half-past three
I throw away my day-disguise,
Become a different Me.

My pouting is quite perfect
My smile becomes a whine;
Admire my transformation
From a pupil once divine.

Why should I clear the table,
Assist with any chore?
My helpfulness is all used up;
There isn't any more!

Yes, meet the secret agent
Who's an undercover double;
At school I am a treasure
And at home I am in trouble!

The Teflon Terror

I know that the monster without a head
Is lying in wait right under my bed
But being headless, he can't see
What I've brought upstairs with me.
This frying pan should do the trick.
BANG!
(I'm glad that monster was non-stick!)

Hadrian's Wall

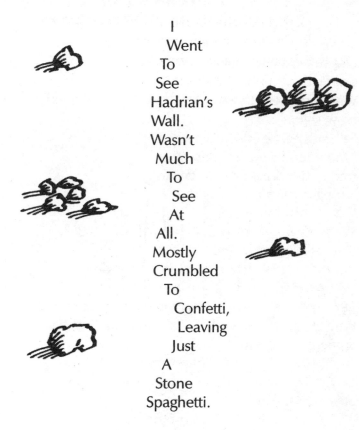

I
Went
To
See
Hadrian's
Wall.
Wasn't
Much
To
See
At
All.
Mostly
Crumbled
To
Confetti,
Leaving
Just
A
Stone
Spaghetti.

Water-Cycle

(A rhythm poem
for acting out or different voices)

Hot sun soak her up,
Cold cloud spit her out,
With a shout of thunder
How she falls.
Falls asleep, lies deep.
Mountains weep and dream
And in the dream she seems to grow,
Stronger, longer,
Full of river-longing
Wide awake, thrills like a milkshake shivers,
She spills into the land.
But then a man-made hand stops her dead
With a dam.
Down, down, down underground, rushing round,
Pushed around by endless fists of metal, how she weeps.
Someone twists the tap.
Tap, kettle, cup of tea, into me and out of me.
Down the drain, underground, rushing round,
Spilling into land
And filling out the sea where the hot sun waits
How she sings!

A Spring Haiku

Buds burst like bullets
The world explodes in colour
Rainfall fans the flames.

Wonder

I wonder at the stars by night,
These little chandeliers of light
I wonder if in turn they see
The tiny spark that makes up me?

I wonder at the hills of green
Rolling like an ocean scene;
As I sail the waves of grass
A whisper says, 'This too shall pass.'

I wonder at the waterfall
Like a silver man so tall,
Singing as he tumbles down,
Wearing Wonder for a crown.

The Pool

We wade through corn like tigers on fire,
And run the obstacle course of barbed wire,
To follow the stream in a winding dream,
Until in a corner, scooped like ice cream,
Under the alders, a hidden pool,
I trail my fingers in the willowy cool.
The grass is bullied and nettles beaten,
Blankets laid for food to be eaten
We leap like salmon, one, two, three,
Dive-bombers of this inland sea,
Hit the water, bodies froze,
Suddenly trout are tickling toes,
The oak is a mast in the ship of shade
Cows drift through the grassy glade
Heads bent like old men reading the news,
As beyond, the hills hold distant views
Under the beaming fat lady sun,
Witch of warmth, conjuring fun,
Until she grows tired and a little bit low,
And daylight packs up, ready to go!
Oh why can't summer last forever,
And why can't we take home this river?
In twilight we stumble through itchy corn,
Get caught on barbed wire with trousers torn,
Sleepily falling into cars
To carry us home under rippling stars.

The Candle

Three in one and one in three
This candle is a trinity.

One for the darkness
Filled with doubt.
Will we ever
Put it out?

Two for the light
So bright and pure.
Pray it shall be
Shadow's cure.

Three for the flickering
Hope we see,
That leads at last
To trinity.

Three in one and one in three
This candle is a trinity.

Snowfall

The paper sky is crumpled white
Filled with opposites of night

Fragments, feathers, falling flakes
Careless crumbs from cloudy cakes

If you are old but dreaming young
Catch a star upon your tongue

If you are young but bright and bold
It's time to sledge the hills of cold.

Mad, Bad and Dangerously Haddock

The umpire gives a wave and they're off
From Sandown at quarter to three,
And the crowd of buoys are going wild,
Bobbing around in the sea.

But the shark's going round in circles!
She's really got no idea,
And Jellyfish is trailing behind,
Hoping to get in the clear.

Tuna thinks it's in the can,
And Salmon's really smokin',
But the shrimps are wimps: no chance in shell!
They really must be jokin'!

Now, Oil is down! She's in a mess!
Oh such spectacular spills,
And the dolphins have lost their porpoise,
While Guppy's fed up to the gills.

The cod are getting battered
Their chips are totally down,
And the fishy scales are tipping,
Now who will win the crown?

Ah, let us toast the sardines,
Who reached the second course,
And the plaice did well in second place,
But the champion of course: Sea Horse!

The Cod Couple

Poor old Cod, all beaten and battered,
Alone on the plate and growing colder.
'It's no fun being a fish!' he fried.
(That Cod had a chip on his shoulder!)

Seagull

Seagull SOars in flight fantastic

Her double rolls are quite gymnastic.

But how she squawks a raucous racket

As on my head, she drops a packet!

California Skateboard Park, 1977

The guys are there,
 I must be good,
  As they can see.
   I take a breath
    And push my board
     Accelerate
      The curving stone
       'Til suddenly
        I reach the top,
         I kick to turn
          To spark my trucks
           And raise a cheer
            For grinding gear.

No time to fear,
  I crouch and pump
    The swooping bowl
      That swallows speed.
        My knees are bent
          To grip the deck
            And leave this earth
              To fly through air,
                A weightless boy
                  Who's earned his wings
                    And every clap;
                      I smoothly land
                        And slide to stop
                          Now out of breath.
                            The guys go 'yeah!'
                              I hear them sing
                                I am the king.

When I Grow Up...

But what if I fall

When I grow up, I want to be as tall as a mountain

O
f
f
?

The Leaf's Lament

Said the leaf to the sky,
'I would learn how to fly,
But I'm shaking like a leaf, do I dare?'

Said the sky to the leaf,
'It's a matter of belief,
Just jump into my blanket of air!'

Then the sky sang,
Then the leaf sprang,
And the trees were empty and bare.

The Moon is on the Microphone
(a country rap)

Oh the trees are dressing for an all-night bop
And the sheep are going bonkers as they do the
   Heron Hop.
And the little leaf sister,
How she boogies with the breeze
As the cows do the rhythm
With the spoons on their knees.
All the birds are singin'
On the Top of the Plops
And the wind he is a drumming
With a bunch of carrot tops.
The sheep are looking chic
In the latest woolly style
As they hop a happy conga
In a crocodile file.
And the stars are driven down
From their mansions in the sky,
The clouds would like a dance
But they dare not even try,
So they cry-baby, hey-baby, grumble and sigh!

And the moon is on the microphone
Crooning quite a tune
As every blade of grass
Is falling to a swoon.
Wow!
What a bop
'Til you drop
In a bucket of slop!
What a sight,
What a night,
What an animal rite!

My Brother the Tree

My brother, a tree so strong, and I
Remember climbing way up high.

My brother, bent over, suddenly sick,
Thin as a twig, snapped like a stick.

My brother, a bonfire built in the dark,
Spitting out one final spark.

My brother, by morning, a cold, grey heap
Curled up in the ash, is this how you sleep?

My brother, a jostle of leaves in my head
Whispering all of the words you said.

My brother, an acorn, a listening ear,
A cup to pour out every fear.

Through all the years you shelter me:
My brother the once and always tree.

By Chance?

Could it only be by chance,
The wonder of your white-night dance?
This shadow I can barely trace –
A shooting star with feathered grace.
Mighty owl, in you I see
An echo of eternity.

Fire at Night

It's ready steady sticks for fiery fun,
The strike of the match is the starter's gun.
Up go the flames, long-jumping sky,
The smoke catches up, hurdling high.
The crowd stamp their frozen feet
Clap their hands for the winning heat.
Guy Fawkes sits on top of the pyre,
Easily beaten, eaten by fire.
Who is quickest in the scorching race?
Flames of gold grab first place.
Who beat the day? The crowd then roars,
The moon made silver to the stars' applause.
Who has come third? No one remembers,
As they all sprint home, leaving only bronze embers.
As clouds shuffle by in a marathon creep,
Children in bed clutch the prize of sleep.

A Winter Haiku

His breath was a cloud
As Jack Frost rode slowly by
On his icicle.

Not What It Seems

One dark night I went to bed
With a nervous sense of dread.
Later, woke to hear a sound
Where such things should not be found:
Whispers deep inside the wall,
And down a non-existent hall,
Footsteps creeping slowly near,
Infecting me with plagues of fear.
Scared, I ran for help next door…
Where wires snaked across the floor
Towards the hi-fi on the shelf.
My brother almost wet himself
My brother shook, was not himself,
And what's worse, to my surprise,
Tears of laughter drowned his eyes.
I traced those wires, found they led
At last to speakers in my bed,
And oh! how hot my tears of shame
Thanks to my brother's ghastly game.

The Mysterious Employment of God

To each and every blade of grass,
Apply a coat of whitest gloss,
Brush the trees (on one side),
Soften hills, far and wide.
Solder horizon, cloud and sky
Make the join invisible to eye.
Windows, wipe with flakes of frost,
Teach smoke to drift, pretend it's lost.
Dress the hedge with spider thread,
Turn to statues flower bed.
Icicles hang at edge of stream,
Allow the hidden buds to dream.

Christmas

This is the tree that was cut down,
This is the smile that was a frown.
This is the angel on top of the bough,
This is the wait all night until now.
This is the day, but what is it for,
As gifts lie scattered all over the floor?
Today, the wrapping is scattered and torn
But there was a baby, wrapped up, newborn.
These are the gifts and that was the birth:
So let us pray for Peace on Earth.

Why Santa has a Smile on His Face

Santa, sick of all that snow,
Has found a better way to go:
If on Christmas Eve it *reins*,
Santa snorkels down the drains!
Between the houses, hear him humming,
As he negotiates the plumbing,
Consults his subterranean maps,
Finally pours out through the taps!
Presents wet? Somewhat unravelled?
Blame the road that Santa travelled.
Modern flats lack chimney breast,
He must simply do his best.
Don't complain and get all whiny,
Just because your present's tiny,
Remember, the object of your gripes
Has cantered through the household pipes,
Oh *deer*, oh *deer*! Don't cause a stink,
When Christmas comes up through the sink.

But when for toys you yelp and yearn,
Pray Santa finds the right-hand turn,
For what once slid down chimney flue,
Might just have struggled through your loo!

Another Sensational Day

The roar of parents,
A curse of clocks;
Tinkle of toilets,
Shrugging on socks.

The flop of cereal,
Pop song of toast;
Hurdling buses,
The bell's mad boast.

The jam of lessons,
As hours overtake;
The theft of daydreams,
The scent of break.

A rush hour of shoes,
The dawdle of light,
A gaggle of gossip
Summoning night.

Excuses for homework,
The glue of the box,
A sinking of pillows…

The curse of clocks.

A Pocket Full of Play

Sing a song of schooltime,
A pocket full of play
Four and twenty children
Working through the day,

When the class was over,
The kids began to sing,
Time for fun and a bucket of sun
Until the bell shall ring.

The kids are in the playground,
Where it's nice and sunny,
Teacher's in the staffroom
Eating bread and honey.

The head is in her office,
Twiddling her toes,
When in came a naughty boy,
Picking at his nose!

My New School

At my new school, I'm a TV.
Everyone stops and stares at me.
I wish I could switch them off.

At my new school, I'm a stone.
If I don't move, they'll leave me alone.
If only I could roll away.

At my new school, I'm a leaf.
I shake all over, with no relief
And a breeze could blow me away.

At my new school, I'm a square.
Why won't the circles and triangles share?
I hate the shape I'm in.

But:

At my new school, I'm a flock of birds,
Listen to all my sing-song words
As my shyness soars away.

At my new school, I'm a football
I bounce from the playground into the hall.
It's great to be part of the team.

At my new school, I'm a pear,
Swinging on the tree with plenty to share
In the season of growing friendships.

At my new school, I'm the Golden Cup,
Winning ideas fill me right up
And my thoughts are a cheering crowd!

Rap Up My Lunch

This is the lunchtime slip slop rap
Spaghetti hoops or sausage in a bap.

Click your fingers, stamp your feet
Groovy gravy, two veg, no meat,

Shake your body, swivel those hips,
Salt and vinegar, fish and chips.

Hold your hands up in the air,
Chocolate custard, apple or pear.

Feel that beat, you're on the loose,
Lemonade or orange juice,

Chatter clatter, make a noise,
No more hungry girls and boys.

Rhythm and rap to the roasting rhyme,
Lunch is done, it's playtime.

Attack of the Mutant Mangos

(a fruit salad ballad of baddies)

They are totally *bananas*
They hang out in a *bunch*,
Don't trifle with these *fruitcakes*
Una-peeling, out to lunch.
They'll *o-range* a nasty accident
And *prune* you down to size,
With hands around your *neck-tarine*
You'll end up in their pies.
They're evil, they're ex-*trawberry*
And rotten to the core,
No more *pudding* up with them;
This is no food fight, it's a war!

Five Little Senses
All in a Row

'You're so sweet!' said Lickety Lips.
'Keep in touch!' said Fingertips.
'See you soon!' said Eye with a wink.
Said the nose, 'Don't cause a stink!'
'Hear me out!' said the ears immense,
'Together, we make a lot of SENSE!'

Playground Chant

Lemon, Larch, Laburnum, Lime,
This is the way we work our rhyme.

Chestnut Sweet and Flowering Cherry,
Today I'm mad, tomorrow merry.

Orange, Olive, Old Man Oak,
Give us a kiss and tell us a joke.

Pomegranate, Prickly Pear,
Does he love me, do I dare?

Beech, Bay, Blackthorn, Box,
Cut off all your curly locks.

Almond, Apple, Ash and Alder,
Will I be famous when I'm older?

Wych Elm, Walnut, Weeping Willow,
Lay your head on sleepy pillow.

Honeysuckle, Hazel, Hornbeam,
Hop to the dance and hope to dream.

Lemon, Larch, Laburnum, Lime,
This is the way we work our rhyme.

The Passionate Pupil
Declaring Love

Come meet with me and after school
Perhaps you'll see that I'm no fool.
If only you would understand,
How I want to hold your hand.

We could walk around the park
Until the day grows old and dark,
And on the swings we'll learn to fly –
Together we will touch the sky,

And I will make a daisy chain,
Create a crown from drops of rain,
Weave a gown of greenest grass
And watch the hours quickly pass.

As we run home through all the streets
I shall give you all my sweets,
The singing of the traffic jam
Will tell you how in love I am.

In class your laughter makes me cry
And I just want to ask you why
You think that I am such a fool
To dream of meeting after school.

Love Poem to Kevin

(he'd better get the message)

Your smile looks like a rip in my jeans,
Your lips resemble an eel,
Your hair has been slurping too much grease,
Can you tell the way that I feel?

Your ears stick up like a pair of forks,
Your hair is greasy spaghetti!
You little squirt of ketchup,
I'd rather snog a yeti!

I Need an Operation on My Pupils!

When we whisper in class
And our desks are a mess,
When we fumble and fidget,
Does it cause you distress?

When we pass little messages
Between every friend,
Forgive us for driving you
Right round the bend!

When we gossip and joke
It's just that we're jolly
And we didn't mean you
To go off your trolley!

Dear teacher, we're sorry,
But we really do care.
And being bald suits you,
Since you've torn out your hair!

Poolside Warriors

We march with armoured duffel bags
Into the palace of echoes,
Chasing enemies with a slip-slap
Through long tiled corridors,
Until we come to the dreaded footbath.
Dragons look on with a glare,
As we launch into the air,
Guided missiles with arms and legs:
Crash, splash and the underwater commandos
Trip and topple unwary targets.
Our floats are U-boats
Ambushing the goggle-eyed adults
Who swim up and down, up and down.

Huge slabs of glass are camouflaged with steam.
With fingers, we trace coded messages of undying love.
The bell goes off like a bomb,
We brave the obstacle course of
Hot and cold showers,
The torture of towel-flicking,
And the tragic death of terrible jokes.
Now weary warriors,
We retreat through frosty streets,
Our breath unfurling
White as the flag of surrender.

Limerlongerick

(with thanks to Gerard Benson)

There was a young bard of Bridport
Who thought limericks were too short.
With all of his art,
He made a start
And went on and on
And on and on
And on and on
And on and on
And on and on
And on and on
And on and on
And on and on
And on and on
And on and on
And on and on
And on and on
And on and on
And on and on
And on and on
And on and on
And on and on
And on and on
As long as he thought he ought.

A Joke too Far

Giggle, jiggle, can't hold back
Crease myself, have a laugh attack.
Split my sides, roll on the floor,
Grin so wide, I could eat a door!

Got the giggles, months of mirth
For the funniest joke on planet earth,
Dying for a laugh, call the Joke Police,
Oops, too late, now I Jest In Peace.

Misadventure

When I am bullied and hard as hate,
I fly away home to my bed.
It is safe as a bank, my golden books
Are treasures that fill up my head.

I close the curtains, banish day,
My bedside lamp is a telescope,
That brings to life the hidden words,
Adventure stories filled with hope.

All my heroes have lots of friends,
And dads who share instead of shout;
The baddies never get their way,
But always end up being found out.

Sometimes, there's a furry dog,
Who jumps from the pages to keep me warm,
Safe with my book in my lonely bed,
And outside the raging storm.

I hate to say goodbye to my friends.
Feel sad at the last full stop.
Tomorrow, I go back to school,
Where the bullies come out on top.

Only We

Only we knew the towering pine tree in the old garden.
Only we egged each other on and gave in to the dare.
Only we found the secret footholds and gripping places.
Only we became breathless as we clambered up.
Only we could look down,
   far down to the black rooftops.
Only we saw the endless chimneys
   poking their noses into the blue.
Only we reached the tip-top
   where branches bent under our weight.
Only we swung like pendulums
   as we screamed at the top of our voices.
Only we prayed not to fall
   as we scratched and tumbled down where
Only we gave silent thanks
   to land back safe on the ground.

A Day in the Life of Me!

Day dawn,
Stretch yawn,
Rise and shine.
Breakfast time,
Mum fuss,
School bus,
Run around
Playground.
Read, write
Tease and fight.
Queue for lunch,
Monster munch.
No surprise.
Time flies,
Half three,
Time for tea
In the park
Until dark.
Quick nosh,
Then wash,
Hamster fed,
Time for bed,
Rain storm,
Bed warm,
Count sheep,
Deep sleep.

The Park

Outside class,
The sun sticks her tongue out, teasing me.
The clock is stuck,
And my head bursts with the future!
At last, the day is done!
My catapult-legs slingshot
Through parent-jams and wailing-baby sirens,
Skitter and skip on still-wet streets,
To the park.

Out of the rush and roar,
Free from the city's mix-and-mash pell-mell,
Behind the rusting gate,
Before the 'don't-be-late',
Is the promised land of Free-Time:

We are explorers,
Laying claim to bushes,
Making dens from shadows,
Playing hide and seek behind
Every second and inside every minute.
We gang up on swings,
Order them to defy gravity
As we dream of looping the loop.
Benches become banquets for sweets
And gossiping words sing like blackbirds.

Up in the trees we are brave as we break
Into stashes of secret sunlight.
At the top, we sway like sailors on lookout,
And far down below
Our park is a green pocket, the place we meet
Zipped up between the grey concrete.

Street Signs

DEAD SLOW CHILDREN
And so I slowed,
Hundreds were crawling
Down the middle of the road!

FORK AHEAD
I rubbed my eyes
A fifty-foot fork
Pronging the skies!
I think I'm going
Round the bend!
There was a sausage
The size of a house
On the end!

HEAVY PLANT CROSSING
I fought with my brolly
As a dastardly daffodil
Said 'give us your lolly!'

A HUMP BRIDGE
Was next, I stopped
with a bump,
The bridge had run off,
It had got the hump!

DIVERSION AHEAD
I'd be home quite soon
First left, then right,
I arrived… on the moon!

The Rubbish Man

I'm the Rubbish Man,
Prince of Plastic, King of Tin Can.
People say that I'm disgusting,
But the children are so trusting
When I rip (or do they throw?)
Such sweet wrappers out of their hands
To scatter them brightly across the lands.

I am the Reveller of Rags,
Emperor of Empty Shopping Bags.

Yes! I'm the Rubbish Man!
Catch me, collar me, collect me if you can.
It's me who stole into your sleep,
Took your mattress soft and deep.
Now, I'm coiled up,
Comfortably rusting by the Rubbish Stream
As she slips her way through the city's dark dream.

Oh! I'm the Rubbish Man!
Rubbing out wishes as only I can.
I made the blocks that burn the sky
And if you dare to ask me why,
I'll say it's my job, it's what I do.
Then will I dance the Rubbish Dance for you.

For I'm the Rubbish Man!
Bin me, bag me, beat me if you can,
But together we'll dance all days away
And darkness, my friend, shall come to stay.

Last Night, I Saw the City Breathing

Last night, I saw the city breathing.
Great gusts of people,
Rushing in and
Puffing out
Of stations' singing mouths.

Last night, I saw the city laughing.
Takeaways got the giggles,
Cinemas split their sides,
And living rooms completely creased themselves!

Last night, I saw the city dancing.
Shadows were cheek to cheek with brick walls,
Trains wiggled their hips all over the place,
And the trees
In the breeze
Put on a show for an audience of windows!

Last night, I saw the city starving.
Snaking avenue smacked her lips
And swallowed seven roundabouts!
Fat office blocks got stuffed with light
And gloated over empty parking lots.

Last night, I saw the city crying.
Cracked windows poured falling stars
And the streets were paved with mirrors.

Last night, I saw the city sleeping.
Roads night-dreamed,
Street lamps quietly boasted,
'When I grow up, I'm going to be a star!'

And the wind,
Like a cat,
Snoozed in the nooks of roofs.

Monstrosity

It has no legs,
It has no arms;
Beware its dark
Metallic charms.

It has no mouth
And yet it cries,
Screaming through
The distant skies.

This beast was never
Born nor bred,
But feel its touch
To join the dead.

A monster? Yes,
The drums now roll
As bomb by bomb
It takes its toll.

The Slippery Truth

Blame the dad
Who bought a bunch.
Blame the girl
Who peeled her lunch.

Blame the bin
That nearly caught it,
Blame the breeze
That flung and fought it.

Blame the boy
Who didn't see
Where it sat
Innocently.

Blame the air
On which he flew
All the way to
Timbuctoo.

But never blame
The trouble he's in
On humble old
Banana skin.

Use Your Rains

(to be read while pinching your nose in
a racing commentator's voice)

The raindrops are quietly gathered in the stalls now,
thundering hooves, pawing the ground,
anxious for the start at the 7.45 from Sundown.
The gun goes off like lightning!
They're off, leaping the first fence in a bunch,
they land in the mud with a splash!
The crowd of crows go wild,
as Bit-Of-A-Drip surges into the lead.
Close behind is Storm-Sausage,
who is on sizzling good form.
But, but, I don't believe it!
Cats'n'Dogs comes bucketing down!
Her owner, Lobelia Completely-Barking
is jumping up and down, cheering her horse on.
It's neck and neck!
The wind is screaming in their ears!
At the last hurdle, the dreadful umbrella jump,
It's impossible! Incredible!
Cloud-Cuckoo-Land drifts into the lead!
Oh! Rain-In-The-Neck is down
and it's Bit-Of-A-Drip, with Home-Sleet-Home,
but in at the finish by the seat of his pants,
at a hundred-to-sun, it's
Soaking-Wet-Bum!

A Poem that Lost Its Briefs

I am a very tiny verse,
Noticed by no one at all,
My ending is unhappy,
Because I am so sma –

Acknowledgments

Unless listed below, the poems in this book have not previously appeared in print. All other poems were first published as credited.

pp. 8, 30, 31, 51, 52, 86, 88 taken from *The Moon Is On The Microphone* by Andrew Fusek Peters, Sherbourne, 1997

pp. 10, 72 taken from *The Unidentified Frying Omelette*, ed. Andrew Fusek Peters, Hodder, 2000

pp. 12, 13, 22, 23, 29, 71, 74, 76, 79, 80 taken from *Sadderday and Funday* by Andrew Fusek Peters and Polly Peters, Hodder, 2001

p. 14 taken from *If The Sea Was In The Sky*, ed. Fiona Waters, Evans Brothers, 2002

p. 15 taken from *On a Camel to the Moon and Other Poems About Journeys*, ed. Valerie Bloom, Belitha Press, 2001

p. 26 taken from *Read Me and Laugh: A Funny Poem for Every Day of the Year*, ed. Gaby Morgan, Macmillan, 2005

p. 34 taken from *Spectacular Spooks*, ed. Brian Moses, Macmillan, 2000

p. 40 taken from *101 Favourite Poems*, ed. John Foster, Collins, 2002

p. 47 taken from *Upside-down Frown: Shape Poems*, ed. Andrew Fusek Peters, Hodder Wayland, 1999

p. 56 taken from *The Horrible Headmonster: A World Book Day Poetry Book*, Macmillan, 2003

p. 60 taken from *Bonkers for Conkers: A World Book Day Poetry Book*, ed. Gaby Morgan, Macmillan, 2003

p. 64 taken from *Sensational!: Poems Inspired by the Five Senses*, ed. Roger McGough, Macmillan, 2004

p. 65 taken from *Why Do We Have To Go To School*, ed. John Foster, Oxford University Press, 2000

pp. 66, 83 taken from *Here Come the Heebie Jeebies and Other Scary Poems*, ed. Tony Bradman, Hodder, 2000

p. 68 taken from *Ready Steady Rap*, ed. John Foster, Oxford University Press, 2001

p. 69 taken from *The Evil Dr Mucus Spleen And Other Superbad Villains*, Macmillan, 2001

p. 70 taken from *The Works: Every Kind of Poem You Will Ever Need for the Literacy Hour*, ed. Paul Cookson, Macmillan, 2000

p. 90 taken from *Wordwhys*, Andrew Fusek Peters, Sherbourne, 1991

p. 93 taken from *The Dog Ate My Bus Pass*, ed. Andrew Fusek Peters and Nick Toczek, Macmillan, 2004

p. 94 taken from *Poems Out Loud*, ed. Brian Moses, Hodder, 2004

p. 95 taken from *Shorts: 100 Poems So Short You Can't Forget Them!*, ed. Paul Cookson, Macmillan, 2000